CONCERT in the SKY

Written and Created by

Joe "The Gamer" Petraro

Pictures by Joe Petraro and Anne Petraro

Fulton Books
Meadville, PA

Published by Fulton Books 2022

ISBN 979-8-88505-573-4 (paperback)
ISBN 979-8-88505-575-8 (hardcover)
ISBN 979-8-88505-574-1 (digital)

Printed in the United States of America

This book is dedicated to all those who have gone to Heaven since the Global pandemic and their loved ones. The world has lost many inspirational people to COVID, addictions, cancers, illness, mental health concerns and suicide. All proceeds from the sale of this book will go to help grievers and anyone dealing with difficult times.

A special dedication of this book is specifically for my friends Jane "Nightbirde" Marczewski and Lilian Callahan. Jane helped me turn closer to Jesus, helped me find confidence and always strive for better through our friendship. She was the driving force to publish this book. I promised her I would and her strength helped me. I miss our chats tremendously. Lilian and I talked throughout the pandemic as she was dealing with an aggressive brain cancer. She was so much fun and a really great artist. I miss my two friends and this book is especially for them.

I woke up and I found out that Jesus had come to get another friend. At first I thought it was a dream but it wasn't. A lot of times when people go to heaven, I sort of hope it's just a dream. I closed my eyes and thought about all the sweet messages I received from my friend and how she always made me feel so much better about things. I thought how happy she must be that Jesus was holding her tight and she was finally home.

I started to think about her family and friends that she talked about so much and I felt really sad for them. I thought about the people that she gave so much hope to and I thought about how many people must be so sad and how many people miss her. At nighttime I cried a lot and talked with Mom to make me feel better. Mom sat with me and let me cry. Crying and listening to music helped me feel better. I thought about all of her loved ones seeing her again one day. I prayed so hard that she would stay on earth. That was my dream. It was her dream too for a long time. Life never goes as planned though and sometimes our dreams still come true but just in a different way. Sometimes God calls people home earlier than we would have liked.

I started to think about all the things that we had spoke about. My friend was a great singer. I imagined so many times sitting in the front row of her sold-out concert watching her sing with her beautiful smile on stage. I told her so many times that I would be at her concert and would never miss it for anything! I told her that she would be fully healed and that I would come to see her. She told me that my books were great and she told me that I was the coolest kid that she had ever met. She told me to keep writing books and I told her that I was going to write a book just for her. This gives me hope and makes me want to do more great things for others in my life. When we lose someone we love, if we think hard about all the great things they did with us and for us, it can be comforting. Even on my worst days she made me realize that a weed was just a beautiful flower that just maybe people didn't realize yet. She made me know that it was OK to be sad and happy at the same time. I'm still going to go to her concert. If I close my eyes I'm there in an instant.

I close my eyes and I mediate and focus on breathing like my Mom taught me. This practice can help a lot of people who feel sad. As I calm down, I feel as if I walk through a thousand perfect clouds. My sadness disappears and I imagine Jesus's embrace just like I would talk about with my friend who went to Heaven. I am in a deep conversation with Jesus about making me feel at peace. I think if we all talk to Jesus like this, He is never very far. I can feel Heaven in this moment and I see a gigantic stage in the clouds. I see a big baby grand piano and a microphone just waiting for someone to sing. The stage looks as if God delicately perfected each and every inch of it. It's as if it is as big as the Heavens. The seats are also as far as the eyes can see. I sit front and center, just like I told my friend I would. I'm all alone. It's the most wonderful thing I've ever looked at. I feel Jesus all along and I thank him for sending me such peace.

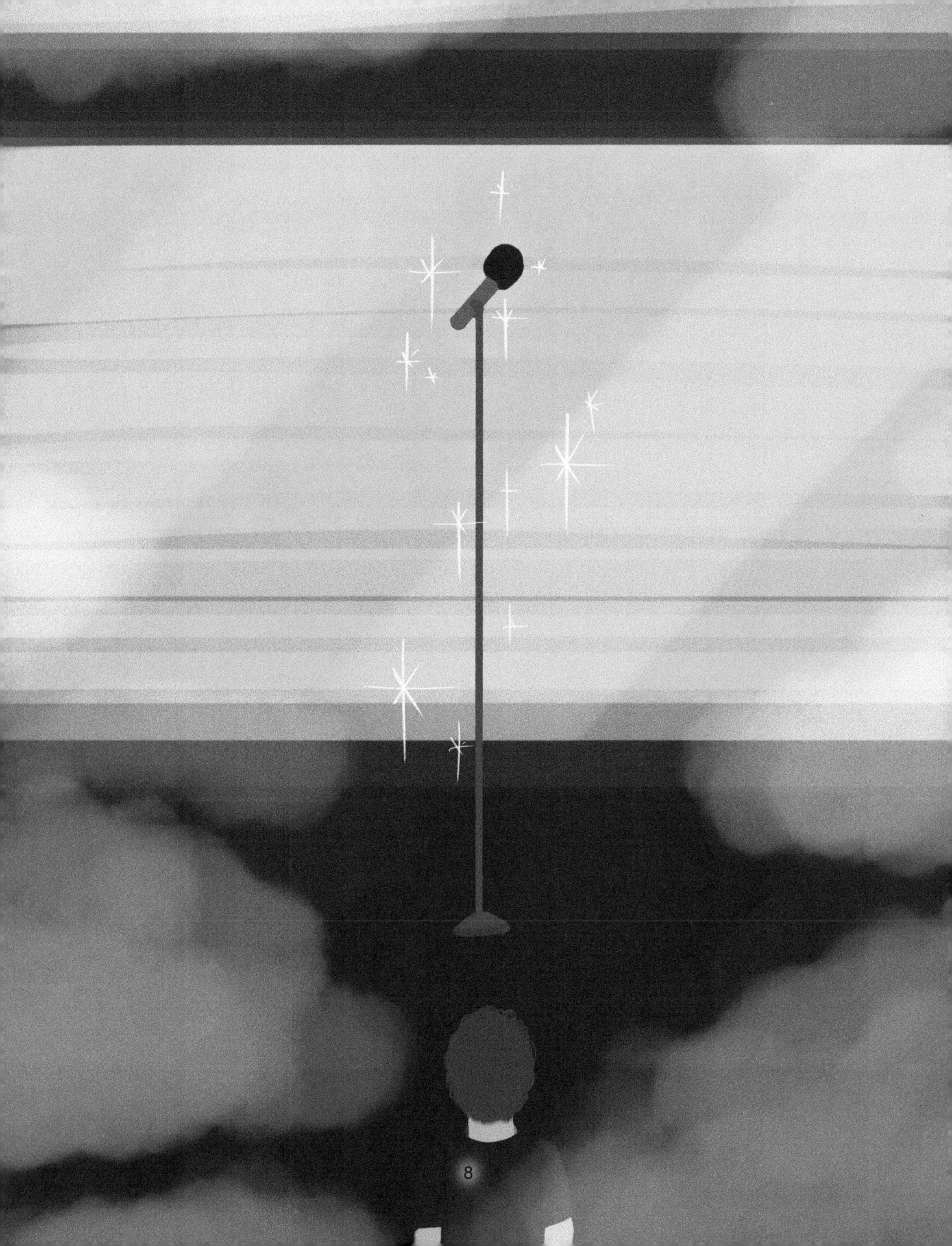

My friend comes onto the stage with such grace. It's like there's a light around her and she looks happier than I've ever seen her which doesn't seem possible because she was always so bright. Even on bad days, she seemed happier than most people. It's just me and my camera and she starts singing. I told her I would sit in the front row of her concert one day and take tons of pictures for her. The song makes me feel good. If I look up over the stage I can see God and all my loved ones who have gone to Heaven. It's a vision I know only God could help me feel. God is with me, even when I'm sad. He sees me through. Now I'm at this beautiful concert in the sky.

She's done singing and in an instant the chairs are full and there's millions and millions of people. I see my Grandma, Grandpa and others who are in Heaven. I see people of all ages running into Heaven to see their family, friends and pets. I imagine all the other people at this concert in the sky are people who are already in God's Kingdom. I think the others are the grievers; all the sad people coming to feel better. People who have gone to Heaven and all their friends are definitely here. Since the pandemic, so many people have gone to Heaven. It's been a hard few years and a lot of people are sad and have big emotions. I think when we are so sad and feel really not great that if we close our eyes and talk to Jesus, he can take us to his Kingdom. Being on Earth can be hard without our loved ones or people like my Grandparents but they aren't very far at all. If we really concentrate hard, we are there. We are all together always; we just need to have faith and talk to God.

I make sure to take so many pictures of the concert in the sky. My mom always taught me pictures are important because they become the moments we look back on and treasure. My friend had big plans before she was saved and went to Heaven—she told me all about them. I know she's still doing everything she said she would, only with Jesus in Heaven. I think humans make a lot of plans and I think it's okay that they don't go according to how they want sometimes. God's plan is so great we can't even understand it here on earth. That's why grief and faith is so hard sometimes. That's why it's important to create our concert in the sky. Maybe it isn't a concert for some people. It can be a nice day at the beach, a dinner with a loved one, or a day at the park with your favorite pet. We can learn to cope with big feelings. I lost a lot of friends recently and for me a concert in the sky is my way of seeing everyone I love and feeling peace in my heart. It takes all the hard emotions and calms them when I need it.

The crowd at the concert in the sky is fabulous. It's like anyone can come to this concert whenever they want. Everyone is full of smiles. People are enjoying their loved ones company. The party in the sky is better than even the best party on Earth! The clouds around the stage and the vision of Heaven is something I know I can take my mind back to whenever I feel upset. I see vivid colors for as far as my eyes can see and I know I'm in Heaven. If I gaze off in the distance I see all of Heaven. It's like there are millions of scenes of peace, lights and love. Heaven is as glorious as the Bible tells us. Everyone I have ever loved and all my pets and all the animals in the world get everything they have ever dreamed of! They are living their dreams! They are saved! The plans they made are even bigger than we can imagine on Earth.

I open my eyes and I'm back on Earth. I feel better now. I know that anyone who is sad can go to their special concert in the sky whenever they want! People who pass away did a lot on earth and they still help us all even though they are with Jesus. We can carry their strength every day. I'm just one little boy who got to meet all these great people who have changed my life. The most recent friend who went to Heaven is just one of millions in the Kingdom of Heaven. People do a lot of good on Earth and sometimes it's hard to understand why babies die, good people can't live longer or why really bad things like pandemics happen. Earth can be hard but it is fun too and we have to try to make the best of it. What's really cool to look forward to is that we all will end up together one day in Heaven! How cool is that?!

I will look for the rainbows on the rainy days. I will keep seeing the weeds as beautiful. I will keep trying to live as those who have passed away did. I know it's ok to be sad and to be human. It's okay to have a really bad day. I also know when I feel bad, all I have to do is talk to God and I can see those who are in Heaven if I close my eyes. I can be happy knowing we had great memories and they are at peace. We all can be sad and feel yucky emotions but it's okay. There's lots of ways to cope that parents, friends and mentors can help us with. Never be afraid to speak up about your grief and sadness because that's how we can all get through sad moments. I like weighted blankets, fidgets and the sound of nature. We all can figure out all different ways to cope. Life can be really hard but we can get through it with each other. After we feel bad we can close our eyes and go to our own concert in the sky. We can all imagine it however we would like!! It is definitely my favorite place to go!

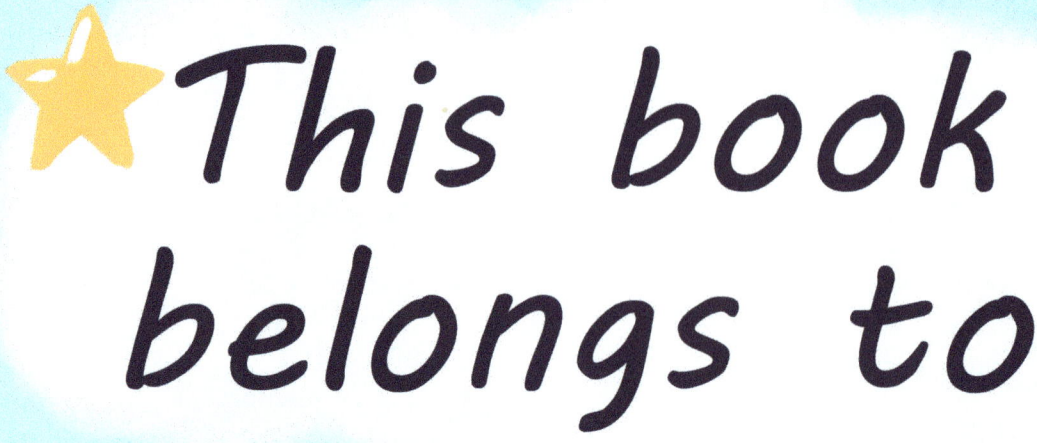

This book belongs to

_____

_____

About the Author

Joseph Petraro is from New York where he resides with his mom, dad, his two dogs Penny and Brady, and his little pet frog. His family is awaiting their new baby vizsla, Gipper. Joseph has been a published author since age six! He attends k12 Private Academy, recently skipped a grade and now is in 5th grade at the age of 9! He keeps close contact with his 3rd grade teacher, Miss Sciortino, who has inspired him a lot and helped him find his way after his old school unexpectedly closed down. She helped him continue writing and journaling through many transitions in his life.

Joseph's creativity to write and express himself through stories has always been a strength of his. Joseph is a very kind young man who has always been a giver since a young age. Joseph is a kid philanthropist who has raised money and given his time for many organizations. In his own community, he started an Adopt-A-Grandparent program, anonymously given to those in need, donated his assets to local educational foundations, people, and charities. When Joseph sees someone in need, he is selfless. Joseph funded a well in Nigeria with his fundraising and book sales which enabled a village to have clean water, live longer, and lets the hospitals have more working equipment. Joseph has a YouTube channel called Joe the Gamer. He has had shirts sponsored from A7 with his logo. These shirts have also helped him raise funds to help others. Joseph is truly a child of God and takes his duty to Jesus very seriously since a very young age.

Joseph fell in love with Jane Marczewski's personality, voice, message, and especially her relationship with Jesus. Although Joseph was younger than Jane, she befriended him and they had conversations about life passions, obstacles, and Jesus. Joseph made a promise his next book would be for Jane and her mission to help others in her situation. Jane's influence on Joseph was huge, and he has now made it his mission to raise all his fundraising efforts to the Nightbirde Foundation.

When Joseph isn't writing or creating books with his mother, Annie, he is very active in many activities. Joseph is a parishioner of St. Raymond Church in East Rockaway, New York where he is an altar boy. He also enjoys music including the violin, drums, singing and piano. Joseph plays travel baseball and basketball in addition to Little League and CYO. He also enjoys tennis, golf, and loves running with his father, Ozzie. Joseph's major passion is karate and he is part of the Warren Levi Dojo in New York. He is also a member in Pack 84 St. Raymond Cub Scouts. Joseph's involvement in martial arts and scouting has contributed to his discipline, ethics, and duty to his community. Joseph has a heart of gold, and his favorite time is time spent with his mom, dad and dogs.

Aside from all Joseph does, he is basically a silly and very humble kid. Seeing him interact with his family and peers, one would never know just how much he does for others. Joseph is a clown and makes everyone laugh. He loves his friends and is truly an example of living how Jesus would. This most recent book is a closer look into Joseph's love of God and how much his friend Jane impacted his life as she did millions of others.